JAM
BEARD'S
POULTRY

JAMES BEARD'S POULTRY

EDITED BY JOHN FERRONE

THAMES AND HUDSON
NEW YORK, NEW YORK

James Beard's recipes and text are adapted from previously published material and are used by permission of Reed College and the executors of his will.

Copyright ©1997 by John Ferrone

First published in the United States of America in paperback in 1997 by Thames and Hudson Inc., 500 Fifth Avenue, New York, New York, 10110

Library of Congress Catalog Card Number 97–60237
ISBN 0–500–27966–7

Designed, typeset and produced by Liz Trovato Book Design
Cover illustration by Patricia Pardini

Printed and bound in Mexico

EDITOR'S NOTE

All of the recipes and much of the text in this cookbook series are James Beard's and are gathered from many sources—magazine articles, syndicated columns, cookbooks, cooking lessons—covering thirty years of culinary exploration. The choice of recipes gives a fair sampling of his thinking on a variety of foods and cuisines. Although he is associated primarily with American cookery, Beard was always on the lookout for gastronomic inspiration in other parts of the world. These cookbooks offer dishes from Portland to Paris, from Maryland to Mexico. Many of them are Beard favorites that turned up in his cooking classes and cookbooks through the years, but also included are less familiar dishes that deserve to be better known. Recipes and text have been edited for these special editions.

BEARD ON POULTRY

ON CHICKEN

What part of the chicken do you enjoy? I have always preferred the dark meat. In former days I cooked chicken so the dark meat would be done to my taste (juicy, with a hint of pink) and then wonder what to do with the light meat, which was invariably overcooked. Well, chicken in parts solved my problem. I can have dark meat to my heart's content. If I want to be very economical, I prepare my own chicken in parts. I buy two or three chickens at a time, cut them up, use the dark meat for broiling and save the light meat for chicken hash or some other dish in which texture and juiciness don't matter that much. Or I freeze the breasts for poaching or for chicken cutlets. I might use the gizzards, hearts, and livers for a sandwich spread. And I often use the legs and thighs to prepare a startling and delicious dish—Chicken with 40 Cloves of Garlic. Everyone who cooks should know how to cut up a chicken.

ON TURKEY

I like fresh-killed turkeys better than frozen ones, but that's purely a matter of choice. They are, to my mind, better flavored, pleasanter to work with, and very often fatter, and they make more agreeable eating. Also, I don't understand people who want small birds. I prefer to roast a bird of 16 to 20 or even 22 pounds, because, I must confess, I still like cold turkey—if it is perfectly cooked. And with a larger bird you get much larger thighs and legs and oysters—those wonderful tidbits that lurk in the backbone and are perhaps the choicest morsels of all.

On Goose

Goose must surely be one of the most neglected and misunderstood of fowl in this country, yet in Europe, since Roman times, it has been regarded as the tenderest and most succulent of all the birds that come to the kitchen. Perhaps this is because American markets have never been able to offer birds of the finest quality. Now, however, we are blessed with golden geese, raised with an eye to tenderness and flavor and then quick-frozen. These are available throughout the country, in sizes from 6 to 12 pounds, with the majority in the 8- to 10-pound range, which means they fit easily into a modern oven and make good sense for a small family. I can testify, as one who has served them for Thanksgiving, that they are extraordinarily fine eating.

On Wild Duck

The cooking of wild duck is a highly individual matter. There are those who cannot stand the sight of blood running in a roasted bird, and there are others to whom a well done duck is unthinkable. Something can be said for both attitudes. I adore underdone duck, but I have a friend who roasts hers, stuffed, for over an hour, and when I eat it I am convinced it is far and away the finest duck I have ever had.

On Pheasant

Although wild pheasant is still available in some parts of the country, compared to past times it is exceedingly rare. However, it is easy enough to buy pheasants raised in captivity. These are the next best thing to the wild birds and sometimes a better bet, as they are usually sold when they are the right age for the oven.

CONTENTS

Chicken

Turkey

Duck and Goose

Pheasant and Quail

CHICKEN

PERFECT ROAST CHICKEN

Serves 4

A simple dish, but one of the best when it is properly cooked. Allow one-quarter chicken for each serving, but you may want to cook an extra chicken to accommodate white-meat or dark-meat eaters. Left-over chicken is never a problem.

4- to 4½-pound roasting chicken
Half a lemon
1 tablespoon fresh tarragon or
 1 teaspoon dried
Salt and freshly ground black pepper
2 strips bacon
2 tablespoons melted butter

Wipe the chicken with a damp cloth, and pat dry with paper towels. Freshen the cavity by rubbing it with the half lemon. Place the tarragon in the cavity. Rub the outside of the chicken with salt and freshly ground black pepper. Place on its side on a rack in a shallow roasting pan. Drape the bacon strips over it. Roast at 400° for 25 minutes. Remove the bacon, turn the chicken on its other side, and brush with melted butter. Return the chicken to the oven to roast for another 25 minutes, and baste again during that time. Turn the chicken breast side up, brush with melted butter and roast for another 30 to 35 minutes, or until the skin is crisp and the legs can be moved easily. Do not overcook. A little pink juice at the joint won't hurt.

Remove the chicken from the oven, and allow the juices to settle for 5 minutes or so before carving the chicken into quarters. Skim off the grease from the pan juices, and spoon the juices over the chicken.

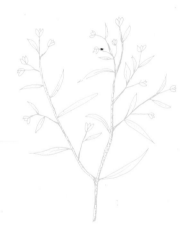

POACHED STUFFED CHICKEN

Serves 4

Poule au Pot, literally "chicken in the pot," is one of the best known of French dishes. Here is an interesting variation that calls for a stuffed chicken.

4- to 5-pound roasting chicken
Chicken liver and gizzard, chopped
½ lemon
½ pound pork sausage meat
2 medium onions, finely chopped
1 clove of garlic, finely chopped
1½ cups dry bread crumbs, plus
*   a dry slice*
1 tablespoon chopped parsley
¼ teaspoon dried thyme
Salt and freshly ground black
*   pepper*
4 egg yolks
1 pound beef shin
1 pound veal neck
Small piece of salt pork or bacon

Freshen the cavity of the chicken by rubbing it with the half lemon. Prepare the stuffing: Gently sauté the sausage meat, breaking it up as it cooks, until it has rendered most of its fat. Pour off the fat. Add the chopped onions and garlic, and cook a few minutes longer. Add the chopped liver and gizzard, bread crumbs, herbs, and a sprinkling of salt and pepper to taste. Mix well, and transfer to a bowl to cool. Add the beaten egg yolks, and blend thoroughly. Stuff the chicken, place the dry slice of bread over the vent and sew up securely. Also tie the neck skin. Then truss the chicken.

Place in a large pot with the beef, veal, and salt pork or bacon. Cover with cold water, add 1½ tablespoons of salt, and bring to a boil. Remove any scum that has formed. Reduce the heat, cover, and simmer for 50 to 60 minutes. Remove the chicken and let it cool. Meanwhile reduce half the broth by one-third over high heat or until it is rich and concentrated. Spoon off any surface fat, and strain the broth. Serve it hot in bowls as a first course. Then serve the cooled chicken and stuffing with a good mustard mayonnaise.

CHICKEN CALANDRIA

Serves 4 to 6

This dish is named for its inventor, an old Mexican cook who used to travel to California to teach her native cuisine. It is a good, spicy buffet dish that benefits from being made ahead and reheated.

4½ - to 5-pound roasting chicken,
*   cut into serving pieces, or its*
*   equal in breasts and legs*
½ cup white water-ground cornmeal
½ cup olive oil
3 medium white onions, finely chopped
3 cloves garlic, finely chopped
¾ cup dry red wine, heated
Pinch each of mace and dried
*   marjoram*
1 teaspoon sesame seeds
½ teaspoon caraway seeds
3 cups boiling water
Salt to taste
1 cup whole blanched almonds
1 cup pitted green olives
4 tablespoons of chili powder or
*   to taste*

Roll the chicken in the cornmeal, shake off the excess, and reserve. Heat the oil in a large casserole, and brown the chicken lightly. Reduce the heat, add the onions and garlic, and allow them to wilt. Then add the wine, mace, marjoram, seeds, and boiling water. Sprinkle with salt. Cover and simmer for 10 minutes. Add the rest of the ingredients and simmer for another half hour.

Mix 3 tablespoons of the reserved cornmeal with ½ cup of cold water, stir it into the sauce, and continue to stir until the sauce has thickened. Serve at once.

If the dish is to be served later, remove it from the heat after it has completed simmering, and allow it to cool. Then reheat and add the cornmeal just before serving.

DJAJ M'KALLI

A subtly flavored Moroccan dish that is served with pickled lemons, which must be made a week or two ahead of time.

Two 3-pound chickens cut in
    serving pieces
2 tablespoons salt mixed with
    3 crushed garlic cloves
1 cup vegetable oil
2 teaspoons ginger
1 teaspoon turmeric
1 teaspoon pepper
Pinch of saffron
3 large onions, grated
1/2 pound butter
3 garlic cloves, chopped
2 cups water
2 cups chicken broth
1 pound ripe olives, preferably
    Calamata
Slices of 2 pickled lemons

Clean the chickens and remove all fat. Rub the skin generously with the salt-garlic mixture. Let stand 1 hour and then wipe off.

Mix the oil with the spices and brush the chicken pieces thoroughly with this. Place in a large pot and pour any remaining oil over them. Refrigerate overnight.

Add the onions, butter, chopped garlic, water, and broth to the pot and bring to a boil over high heat. Reduce the heat and simmer until the chicken is tender, about 40 to 45 minutes. Remove the chicken from the pot and set aside. Reduce the liquid in the pot over high heat, stirring often, until it forms a thick, rich sauce. Skim off excess fat. Add the olives and the lemon slices. Return the chicken to the pot, and simmer for about 10 minutes to reheat. Place on a large platter around rice with pine nuts, or couscous.

PICKLED LEMONS

8 large lemons
½ cup coarse salt
Olive oil to cover (or half olive oil,
half peanut oil)

Slice the lemons ¼ inch thick and place in a colander. Sprinkle heavily with salt and cover with plastic wrap. Place over a bowl and allow to drain for 24 hours.

Rinse well, then pack into jars with oil to cover. Seal and let stand for one to two weeks before using, by which time the lemons will have softened and mellowed in taste. It may be necessary to add salt after the lemons have ripened—1 tablespoon per jar. They will keep indefinitely if immersed in oil.

POULET VALLÉE D'AUGE

Serves 4

A recipe that does credit to its Norman ancestry, with its combination of cream, Calvados, cider and apples.

3½- to 4-pound chicken, cut in quarters

Flour

4 tablespoons lard

1 teaspoon salt

½ teaspoon freshly ground black pepper

6 good-sized cooking apples, peeled and thinly sliced

7 tablespoons butter

2 tablespoons sugar

½ cup dry cider or dry white wine

¼ cup Calvados or applejack

1½ cups light cream

Crisp toast

Dust the chicken pieces with flour and shake off the excess. Heat the lard in a large skillet and brown the chicken well on all sides. Sprinkle with salt and pepper. Add the cider or wine to the pan, cover, and simmer the chicken for 20 minutes or until tender.

Meanwhile prepare the apples. Heat 4 tablespoons of butter in another skillet, add the apples, and sauté over low heat for 2 minutes or so. Sprinkle with the sugar, and cook for 3 minutes more. Set aside.

When the chicken is done, uncover, pour in the Calvados or applejack and carefully ignite. After the flaming has stopped, transfer the chicken to a hot platter. Knead the remaining butter with 3 tablespoons of flour, and stir into the juices in the pan. Continue stirring over low heat while adding the cream until thickened and smooth. Place the chicken quarters on the toast and pour the sauce over them. Serve with the sautéed apples.

CHICKEN PANNÉ

Serves 8

In this luscious recipe the chicken breasts are pounded as thin as veal scallopine and cooked just as quickly, leaving the coating nicely browned and the interior still juicy.

4 whole boneless and skinless
    chicken breasts, cut in half
1 cup flour
2 eggs, lightly beaten
3 cups fresh bread crumbs
6 tablespoons butter
Salt and freshly ground black pepper
3 tablespoons cognac, warmed
1 cup cream, blended with 2 egg yolks

Pound the chicken breasts between sheets of wax paper until uniform in thickness, about ⅛ inch. Dredge in the flour, dip in the beaten egg, and press into the bread crumbs to thoroughly coat. As the pieces are done, transfer them to a plate and separate with wax paper to keep from sticking. Refrigerate for an hour or more to firm the coating.

To cook, heat the butter in a large skillet until bubbling hot but not browning. Reduce the heat to medium, and sauté the chicken breasts, two at a time, for a minute or so on both sides until browned. Sprinkle with salt and pepper and transfer to a hot platter. Then return the pieces to the pan and flame them (off-heat) with the cognac. Again transfer to a hot platter while you make the sauce: Add the cream and egg mixture to the pan and stir over medium heat until slightly thickened, but do not allow to boil. Add salt and pepper to taste and serve with the chicken.

MININA

An unusual Egyptian dish of chicken, brains, and eggs, baked and served like a frittata.

½ pound calf's brains

Juice of ½ lemon

2½ teaspoons salt

1 pound chicken breasts

9 eggs

⅛ teaspoon nutmeg

*½ teaspoon freshly ground black
    pepper*

3 hard-boiled eggs, finely chopped

4 tablespoons peanut oil

Lemon wedges

Soak the brains in cold water to cover for about an hour. Remove the membrane and trim the base. Put in a pan of cold water to cover, and add the lemon juice and ½ teaspoon of salt. Bring to a boil and simmer 5 to 7 minutes. Drain and dry well, then cut into small pieces.

Place the chicken breasts in a shallow pan with water to cover and 1 teaspoon of salt. Bring to a boil, remove any scum, and reduce the heat. Simmer for about 12 minutes. Drain off the liquid and reserve. Remove the skin and bones from the chicken, and cut the meat into strips 1 inch long and ½ inch wide.

Beat the eggs well, and add

the nutmeg, the remaining salt, and the pepper. Add the brains, chicken, and hard-boiled eggs, and mix gently. In a 12-inch skillet that can go into the oven heat the oil until very hot. Add the egg mixture, and bake in a 350° oven for 15 minutes, or until a knife inserted in the center comes out clean. Invert onto a platter, sprinkle with about ¼ of the reserved chicken broth, and surround with the pieces of lemon. To serve, cut in wedges.

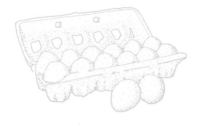

POULET AU VINAIGRE

Serves 4

Vinegar gives this dish its special distinction, and it can be any of the flavored vinegars we find in our markets today, including those touched with raspberries, strawberries, blueberries, or black currants; vinegars made from sherry, Madeira or champagne; or vinegars infused with herbs and seasonings

3-pound chicken, cut in quarters
4 tablespoons unsalted butter
1 tablespoon olive oil
Salt and freshly ground black pepper
6 garlic cloves, unpeeled
½ cup white wine
½ cup wine vinegar
½ cup Armagnac
1 teaspoon Dijon mustard
1 teaspoon tomato paste
½ cup plus 1 tablespoon crème fraîche
2 tomatoes, peeled, seeded and coarsely chopped
1 teaspoon fresh tarragon, finely chopped

Heat 2 tablespoons of butter and the olive oil in a heavy sauté pan, and sear the chicken until lightly colored, approximately 5 minutes on each side. Season with salt and pepper. Add the garlic cloves. Cover the pan and simmer for 10 minutes. Remove the cover and continue cooking the breast quarters for another 10 minutes, turning once, and remove to a platter. Cook the leg quarters 5 minutes more (15 minutes altogether) and remove also. Do not overcook. Pour off ½ of the fat. Add the wine and deglaze the pan. Reduce over moderate heat by ½.

Mix the wine vinegar,

Armagnac, mustard and tomato paste together in a small bowl. Add to the pan along with ½ cup of crème fraîche. Cook slightly to thicken. Then stir the remaining crème fraîche and butter into the sauce. Taste for seasoning. Pour the sauce on a serving platter, arrange the chicken quarters on the sauce, and garnish with the chopped tomato and tarragon.

Note: Crème fraîche is matured cream that has been allowed to thicken naturally. If it is not available, substitute heavy cream, though it will not have the same nutty flavor or consistency. Do not substitute sour cream.

MUSTARD CHICKEN

Serves 4

This is a simple but splendid dish. The cream gives the sauce a lovely texture, and as it cooks with the mustard it thickens a little more.

4 large chicken breast halves
2 tablespoons flour
4 tablespoons butter
2 tablespoons oil
Dijon or herbed mustard
1 medium onion, finely chopped
½ cup mushrooms, finely chopped
2 tablespoons chopped parsley
Salt and freshly ground black pepper
1 cup heavy cream
1 teaspoon lemon juice

Dust the chicken lightly with flour. Heat the butter and oil in a skillet, and sauté the chicken until browned on all sides. Transfer to a shallow baking dish, and spread each piece of chicken liberally with mustard. In the fat remaining in the skillet, sauté the onions until they begin to color, then add the mushrooms and cook until tender. Add the parsley and a sprinkling of salt and pepper. Blend in the cream and stir until heated through. Pour over the chicken. Bake uncovered at 350° for 30 to 35 minutes. Stir the lemon juice into the sauce and taste for seasoning. Serve with plain white rice.

CHICKEN WITH 40 CLOVES OF GARLIC

Serves 8

A Provençal recipe that never fails to astonish, but slow braising gives the garlic a delicate flavor.

⅔ cup olive oil

8 chicken drumsticks

8 chicken thighs

4 ribs celery, cut in long strips

2 medium onions, chopped

6 sprigs parsley

1 tablespoon chopped fresh tarragon
    or 1 teaspoon dried

½ cup dry vermouth

2½ teaspoons salt

¼ teaspoon freshly ground black
    pepper

Dash of nutmeg

40 cloves of garlic, unpeeled

French bread or toast

Pour the oil into a shallow dish, add the chicken parts, and turn to coat all sides. In a heavy 6-quart casserole combine the celery, onions, parsley, and tarragon. Arrange the chicken on top, pour in the vermouth, and sprinkle with salt, pepper, and nutmeg. Tuck the garlic cloves among the chicken pieces. Cover the casserole tightly with foil, and put on the lid. Bake at 375° for 1½ hours.

Serve the chicken with the pan juices, whole garlic cloves and slices of heated French bread or toast. Squeeze the garlic out of its skin from the root end onto the bread, and spread like butter.

CHICKEN LEGS WITH WALNUTS

Serves 4 to 6

A quick, inexpensive dish but fancy enough for a dinner party. Serve with rice pilaf.

6 whole chicken legs
3 tablespoons each butter and oil
1 small onion, finely chopped
1 cup walnuts, finely chopped
1 cup chicken broth
Salt and freshly ground black pepper
    to taste
¼ cup chopped parsley
¼ cup toasted walnut halves

In a large skillet sauté the chicken legs in butter and oil until nicely browned on all sides. Add the onion, chopped walnuts and broth. Cover and simmer 20 minutes or until the chicken is tender, turning once. Season with salt and pepper. Sprinkle each serving with chopped parsley and walnut halves.

So See Gai
(Chicken and Coriander Salad)

Serves 6

Here is a delicious chicken salad that is dominated by the flavor of fresh coriander or Chinese parsley, which can be found in Chinese markets or in Hispanic markets, where it is known as cilantro, and is becoming more generally available.

1 fully roasted 4½- to 5-pound chicken

1 tablespoon hot Chinese mustard

1 to 2 tablespoons sesame seeds, toasted in a 375° oven

6 to 8 green onions, finely shredded lengthwise and cut into 1½-inch pieces

1 bunch fresh coriander, washed and dried

1½ teaspoons salt

⅛ teaspoon sugar

½ teaspoon monosodium glutamate (optional)

½ head of iceberg lettuce, very finely shredded

Allow the roasted chicken to cool, then strip the meat from the bones. Pull into fine shreds with your fingers, and put into a bowl. Add the mustard and mix. Then add the toasted sesame seeds and green onions. Strip the leaves from the coriander stalks, saving a few whole ones for a garnish. Add to the chicken along with the salt, sugar, and monosodium glutamate. Toss together well. Line a platter with the shredded lettuce, arrange the chicken salad on top, and garnish with the sprigs of coriander.

CHICKEN HASH

Serves 4

Chicken hash has always been a favorite in America. There must be a million different versions. Whatever you make it with, a good hash is a joy, and one of the best ways to make a simply wonderful meal out of leftovers.

4 tablespoons butter or part butter,
    part chicken fat
1 large onion, finely chopped
5 small cooked potatoes, diced
1/4 teaspoon rosemary, crumbled
Salt and freshly ground black pepper
2 1/2 cups cooked chicken, cut into
    large dice
2 or 3 cooked gizzards, finely
    chopped (optional)
1/4 cup chicken broth or gravy
1/3 cup heavy cream
1/2 cup chopped parsley

Heat the butter in a skillet and sauté the chopped onion until it begins to color. Mix in the diced potatoes, and cook a few minutes longer. Sprinkle with the rosemary and salt and pepper to taste. Mix the chicken and gizzards with the broth or gravy, and fold into the potato-onion mixture. Cook gently for 5 minutes. Pour in the heavy cream, and let that cook down. By this time the bottom of the hash should be nice and brown. Fold in the chopped parsley. Serve good and hot with a green salad.

VARIATIONS:

1. Add 1/2 cup finely chopped sautéed mushrooms.

2. Add 1/4 cup toasted almonds at the last minute.

3. Omit the heavy cream and off heat stir in 2 beaten egg yolks instead. Sprinkle the top with grated Parmesan cheese and run it under the broiler for a few minutes to lightly brown.

TURKEY

ROAST TURKEY WITH RICE-PISTACHIO STUFFING

This unusual stuffing can be adjusted to fit a larger or smaller bird. For a 20- to 24-pound turkey increase the rice to 10 cups; for a 9-pound turkey reduce the rice to 5 cups; and adjust the remaining ingredients proportionately.

16-pound turkey

FOR THE STUFFING:
8 cups cooked rice (2 to 2²/3 cups
*   raw, depending on type of rice)*
1 1/2 cups green onions
4 tablespoons butter
1 cup finely chopped parsley
2 cups finely chopped cooked ham
1 cup pistachio nuts
2 teaspoons dried tarragon
Salt and freshly ground black
*   pepper*
3/4 cup butter, melted
1/2 cup sherry or Madeira

FOR BASTING:
Oil and melted butter, mixed;
*   or strips of salt pork or bacon;*
*   or melted butter and white*
*   wine, mixed*

Rub the cavity of the turkey with a half lemon before stuffing. Cook your favorite rice, and while it is still warm, toss it lightly with 3 or 4 tablespoons of oil to keep the grains separated. Gently sauté the green onions in the butter, and add the rice, parsley, ham, nuts, tarragon, and salt and pepper to taste. Finally blend in the melted butter and sherry or Madeira. Taste for seasoning.

Stuff the turkey loosely with this mixture and close the vent by fitting a double thickness of foil over the stuffing, using metal skewers, or sewing with needle and twine. Secure the neck skin to the back with a skewer. Cut off the wing tips. Truss the entire bird. Rub the skin with butter or oil and sprinkle with salt and pepper. Place the turkey on its side on a rack in a shallow pan. To keep it moist during cooking, you can cover the breast and legs with well-oiled cheesecloth and baste through the cheesecloth with oil and melted butter; or cover with strips of salt pork or bacon and baste occasionally with the pan juices; or butter the bird lavishly and baste with a mixture of half melted butter and half white wine.

It is impossible to give exact timings for roasting a turkey, but a bird of this size will take approximately 3 to 3½ hours at 325°. After ⅓ of the cooking time, turn the bird on its other side (using a wad of paper towels), and after another ⅓ turn it breast side up. If the skin starts to brown too much, cover it loosely with a foil tent until done. Test by moving a leg to see whether it gives easily; the drumstick and breast meat should feel soft when pressed with the fingers; and a thermometer thrust into the thigh without touching the bone should register about 170°. Remove from the oven and let stand 20 to 30 minutes before carving.

BROILED YOUNG TURKEY

Serves 4

Only very young, fresh-killed turkeys broil successfully. Split the turkey and remove the breastbone and backbone before soaking in the marinade.

3½- to 5-pound fresh turkey
1 cup white wine
½ cup Japanese soy sauce
3 garlic cloves, finely chopped
¼ cup olive oil
1 tablespoon Tabasco

Place the turkey in a shallow roasting pan. Combine the rest of the ingredients and pour over the turkey. Allow to marinate for an hour or more, turning several times. Transfer to a broiling pan and place 4 to 5 inches from the source of heat.

Broil bone side to the heat for about 25 minutes, basting occasionally with the marinade. Turn, brush with marinade, and broil until nicely browned and cooked through, about 18 to 25 minutes more. Be careful not to overcook, or the white meat will be dry and uninteresting. Serve with fried rice.

ROAST TURKEY BREAST WITH TARRAGON SAUCE

Serves 8

If you do not want to deal with a big bird, and no one will miss the dark meat, here is a nice solution.

1 whole turkey breast, 7 to 8 pounds
½ cup each melted butter and
    white wine
Salt and freshly ground black
    pepper

Place the breast, skin side up, on a rack in a shallow roasting pan, and brush with the butter-wine mixture. Sprinkle with salt and pepper. Roast at 350°, allowing 20 minutes per pound or until an internal temperature of 170° is reached. Baste with the butter and wine every half hour. When done, remove the turkey from the oven and allow to rest 15 to 20 minutes before carving. Serve with the tarragon sauce.

TARRAGON SAUCE

5 tablespoons butter

3 tablespoons minced onion

4 tablespoons flour

1½ cups turkey or chicken broth

Salt and freshly ground black
    pepper

1½ teaspoons dried tarragon or
    1 tablespoon fresh, chopped

½ cup heavy cream

Melt the butter in a heavy saucepan over medium heat, add the onion, and cook gently until tender but not brown. Stir in the flour and cook for another minute or so, then stir in the broth, and continue to cook until smooth and thickened. Reduce the heat, and add the tarragon. Gradually add the heavy cream, and cook until well blended. Taste for seasoning, and add salt and pepper, if needed.

TURKEY MOLE

Serves 4

One of the simpler versions of this most traditional of Mexican dishes.

*1 turkey breast and wing, about
    3 to 4 pounds*
1½ teaspoon salt
2 medium onions, chopped
Bacon fat or oil
2 cloves garlic
2 tablespoons chili powder
1 small dried red chili pepper
*1 cup ground nuts—almonds,
    walnuts, peanuts, or cashews*
2 ounces bitter chocolate
1 cup ripe olives (optional)

Cut the turkey wing into 2 pieces and the breast into 3 or 4 pieces. Place in a large pot with enough water to cover, and bring to a boil. Add the salt, and simmer for 30 minutes. Meanwhile brown the onion in bacon fat or oil. Add to the pot, along with the garlic, chili powder, red pepper, nuts, and chocolate. Cover and simmer until the turkey is tender and the sauce is well blended and thickened. Taste for salt. Add the olives about 10 minutes before serving. Serve with polenta and a cucumber salad.

TURKEY CHILI

Serves 8 to 10

Not a traditional dish but an experiment that turned out to be delicious. It is an excellent choice for a buffet party, served with tortillas, rice or polenta and a cucumber and radish salad.

5 to 6 pounds turkey thighs
2 ribs celery
2 sprigs parsley
2 small dried hot peppers
1 medium onion stuck with 2 cloves
Water
Salt
2 tablespoons chili powder, or
to taste
1 4-ounce can chopped green chilies
1 cup ground almonds
1/2 cup ground peanuts
1 large onion, finely chopped
3 cloves garlic, finely chopped
2 green peppers, finely chopped
1/4 cup olive or peanut oil
1 cup small pitted green olives
1/2 cup blanched almonds

Place the turkey in a large casserole with the celery, parsley, hot peppers, onion, and water to cover. Bring to a boil, remove any scum that forms, and add 1 tablespoon of salt. Reduce the heat, cover, and simmer about 1 hour or until the meat is tender but not falling from the bones. Remove the turkey from the broth and set aside.

When cool enough to handle, strip off the meat in large chunks, discarding the bones and skin. Strain the broth and skim off excess fat. Then reduce over high heat to about 4 cups. Taste for salt. Stir in the chili powder, green chilies, ground almonds, and peanuts. Simmer about 10 minutes, stirring occasionally, or until the sauce has thickened.

In a skillet sauté the onion, garlic, and peppers in oil until tender. Add to the sauce, and simmer another 5 minutes. Add the turkey meat and heat through. Finally add the olives and almonds, and cook another 3 minutes.

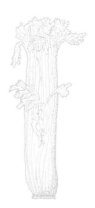

TURKEY BREAST PAPPAGALLO

Serves 6

Turkey is treated much like veal scallopine in this recipe and is just as delicious. If your butcher cannot provide turkey cutlets, you can easily prepare them yourself by slicing a partly thawed frozen turkey breast.

12 slices turkey breast ⅜ inch thick
Flour
12 tablespoons butter
6 tablespoons oil
Salt and freshly ground black pepper
12 slices of ham
1 cup sliced mushrooms lightly
* sautéed in butter*
Turkey or chicken broth
Freshly grated Parmesan cheese
Chopped parsley

Pound the turkey slices between sheets of wax paper until ¼ to ⅛ inch thick. Dust the slices with flour. Heat the butter and oil in two skillets, and quickly sauté the turkey on both sides. This may have to be done in batches. Sprinkle with salt and pepper. Top each turkey slice with a slice of ham and a tablespoon of mushrooms. Spoon a little broth over all, and sprinkle with Parmesan cheese. Reduce the heat to a simmer, cover the pans and cook until the cheese melts, about five minutes. Transfer the turkey to a hot platter, spoon the juices over, and sprinkle with chopped parsley.

TURKEY TONNATO

If you happen to be roasting a turkey breast for one hot meal, then use the leftovers, instead of veal, for this version of Vitello Tonnato. Or do a small turkey breast just for this dish.

4- to 4½-pound turkey breast,
    fresh or frozen
5 or 6 anchovies
1 garlic clove, slivered
4 tablespoons melted butter, mixed
    with ½ cup white wine
2 cups mayonnaise
1 cup finely flaked dark tuna
1 garlic clove, finely chopped
2 tablespoons finely chopped parsley
2 hard-cooked eggs, sliced or quartered

Loosen the skin on the turkey breast and slip the anchovies underneath. Make incisions in the meat with a small knife and stud with garlic slivers, as you would do for a leg of lamb. Roast in a 350° oven, allowing 20 minutes a pound, or until it reaches an internal temperature of 160 to 165°, basting several times with the butter-wine mixture. When done, allow to cool.

Remove the breast meat from the bone, and sample a piece for salt; the anchovies should have provided enough. Cut the meat in neat, thinnish slices. Mix the tuna with the mayonnaise, and add the chopped garlic and parsley. Spread each slice of turkey with the mayonnaise and arrange on a serving dish. Garnish with the slices of quartered eggs. Serve with a rice salad.

TURKEY IN LETTUCE LEAVES

Serves 10 to 12

This is an unusual first course, because hot turkey is eaten in icy-cold lettuce leaves. Guests spoon some of the filling on the lettuce, roll it up and eat it with the fingers like a taco. The contrast between the crisp, icy lettuce and the hot, spicy filling is unbelievably delicious.

6 tablespoons butter

2 cups finely chopped onion

¾ cup finely chopped green pepper

4-ounce can chopped green chili peppers, drained

1 to 2 tablespoons fresh hot chili pepper, finely chopped

4 cups finely diced turkey

2 tablespoons chopped fresh basil or 1½ teaspoons dried

1 teaspoon salt or to taste

½ teaspoon freshly ground black pepper

⅓ cup cognac

½ cup turkey or chicken broth (optional)

¼ cup chopped parsley

¾ cup shaved toasted almonds

2 to 3 heads well-chilled iceberg lettuce, separated into leaves

Melt the butter in a large skillet and sauté the onion and pepper until wilted. Add the green and hot chili peppers and the turkey, and toss well. Cover and simmer 5 minutes. Add the basil, salt and pepper, and cognac. If the mixture seems too dry, add up to ½ cup of broth. Taste for seasoning. Transfer to a large heated bowl or casserole, and garnish with the chopped parsley and toasted almonds.

Arrange the lettuce leaves in piles on a large platter and place next to the bowl of filling. To eat, spoon some filling on a lettuce leaf and roll it up loosely. No knives or forks are required.

TURKEY SOUFFLÉ

Serves 4

An elegant way to use up a bit of leftover turkey.

4 tablespoons butter

3 tablespoons flour

1 cup turkey broth or milk

1 teaspoon salt

½ teaspoon freshly ground black pepper

⅛ teaspoon nutmeg

4 egg yolks, beaten

1 cup ground cooked turkey

4 egg whites, beaten until stiff but not dry

In the top of a double boiler, over boiling water, blend together the butter and flour to make a roux, and cook for about 2 minutes. Stir in the broth or milk and continue stirring until thickened. Season with salt, pepper, and nutmeg. Remove from the heat and when slightly cooled, beat in the egg yolks. Add the turkey and blend well. Finally fold in the beaten whites. Pour into a greased 1½-quart soufflé dish and bake at 400° for 25 to 35 minutes. Serve with a béchamel sauce.

DUCK AND GOOSE

ROAST DUCKLING AU POIVRE

Serves 2

Duck takes nicely to this peppery treatment, based on the same idea as Steak au Poivre.

4- to 5-pound duckling
Salt
Dried thyme or rosemary
1 onion, stuck with 2 cloves
1 tablespoon crushed black peppercorns

Rub the skin of the duckling with salt and the herb of your choice. Put the onion in the cavity.

Arrange on a rack in a shallow roasting pan. Roast at 350° 1½ hours for medium-rare duck and 2 hours for well-done. After the first half-hour prick the skin with a fork all over to release the fat, and repeat the process. Half an hour before the duck is done, remove it from the oven and press the peppercorns into the skin. Return it to the oven to fin-ish roasting. For a really crisp duck, increase the heat to 500° for the final 15 minutes. To test for doneness, prick the thigh joint to release a bit of juice. Pink juice indicates medium-rare; clear juice, well-done. To serve, cut the duck into halves or quarters with poultry shears.

ROAST WILD DUCK

Since no two cooks can agree on the proper cooking time for wild duck, it is a matter of individual taste—running from a rare bird to one that is falling off the bone. Count on serving half a duck per person, unless the duck is small, in which case you'll need one per person.

FOR EACH DUCK:

A few juniper berries or a pinch
  of thyme
Butter
Olive oil
2 tablespoons melted butter mixed
  with 2 tablespoons red wine,
  port or Madeira
Salt and freshly ground black pepper

Put the juniper berries or thyme and 1 tablespoon of butter in the cavity of the bird. Rub the skin well with butter or olive oil, and arrange on a rack in a roasting pan. For rare duck, roast in a 450° oven for 17 to 18 minutes, basting once or twice with the melted butter and wine. Season with salt and pepper.

For better done duck, roast at 450° for 20 minutes, then reduce the heat to 350° and continue to roast, basting frequently, to the preferred state of doneness—but not more than 45 minutes in all.

BROILED DUCK
TERIYAKI

Serves 2

4- to 5-pound duck, split
1/2 cup soy sauce
1/2 cup white wine, sherry or sake
1 to 2 tablespoons fresh chopped
    ginger root or 1 teaspoon
    ground ginger
1 or 2 chopped garlic cloves
1 teaspoon grated orange rind or
    1 tablespoon tangerine rind strips
1/4 cup peanut oil

Place the duck in a glass, enameled or stainless steel container. Mix the rest of the ingredients together and pour over the duck. Refrigerate for 1 to 24 hours, turning the duck in the marinade several times during that period. When ready to cook, remove from the marinade and drain well.

If broiling over charcoal, place on a grill 6 to 7 inches from the coals that are not too hot. If broiling in the oven, place on a rack about 5 inches from the source of heat. Starting with the bone side to the heat, broil slowly about 15 minutes, then turn and broil for about 10 minutes on the other side. Test for doneness by pricking the bird to see if the juices run pink or clear.

The duck can be brushed with the marinade as it cooks, but if it has marinated overnight it probably needs no further flavoring.

DUCK AND RED CABBAGE CASSEROLE

Serves 2 to 4

This savory duck casserole would be nicely complemented by crisp potato pancakes.

5-pound duck, cut into quarters
Flour
Salt and freshly ground black pepper
6 tablespoons butter or oil
1 medium onion, finely chopped
1 teaspoon caraway seeds, crushed
Pinch dried basil
½ cup white wine
1 medium head red cabbage, shredded,
    discarding the hard core
3 tablespoons wine vinegar
2 tablespoons brown sugar

Dredge the duck quarters in flour and salt and pepper, and brown in a skillet in 4 tablespoons of butter or oil. Remove the duck and drain well of fat. Arrange in an ovenproof casserole. Add the chopped onion, caraway seeds, basil, and wine. Cover and bake at 350° for half an hour.

Meanwhile heat the remaining butter or oil in the skillet, add the cabbage, and cook down over moderate heat for 10 minutes, tossing it as it cooks. Add the wine vinegar, brown sugar, and a sprinkling of salt and pepper. Reduce the heat and simmer another 5 minutes. Spoon over the duck in the casserole, cover, and bake until the duck is tender, about 1 hour.

TERRINE OF DUCKLING

Serves 2 to 4

A dish that requires time and work but makes an impressive presentation for an elegant dinner party or buffet.

One 4-pound duckling, skin removed
    and reserved
Small strip pork skin
1 leek, well cleaned
1 sprig fresh thyme or 1/2 teaspoon dried
1 stalk celery
1 bay leaf
4 cups chicken broth
1 pound chicken livers
1 pound lean pork
6 shallots, peeled
1 garlic clove, peeled
1/4 cup chopped parsley
5 eggs
1 tablespoon flour
1 1/2 teaspoons salt
1/2 teaspoon pepper
3/4 cup cognac
1 pound cooked tongue, cut in thin
    strips
Sliced truffles (as much as you
    can afford)

1/4 pound larding pork, thinly sliced
1 envelope plain gelatin, softened in
    1/4 cup cold water

Cut the meat from the duck, and set aside the breast pieces. Place the bones, neck, gizzard, and heart (reserve the liver) in a large kettle, along with pork skin, leek, thyme, celery, and bay leaf. Add the chicken broth and enough water to immerse the bones. Cover and bring to a boil. Simmer for 2 hours.

Put the duck meat (except for the breast), duck liver, chicken livers, and pork through a food chopper, together with the shallots, garlic, and parsley. Add the eggs, one at a time, pounding in well with mortar and pestle or in a heavy bowl with a wooden spoon. Or grind in a food processor in 2 or 3 batches. Sprinkle in the flour, salt, pepper, and cognac, and blend thoroughly.

Line the bottom of a large oval terrine or 2½-quart casserole with the duck skin. Add half of the meat mixture, and press in evenly. Arrange the duck breast, strips of tongue, and sliced truffles over this. Add the rest of the meat. Top with the strips of larding pork. Bake, uncovered, at 300° for 2½ hours.

Remove the cover from the pot of broth, and reduce it over high heat to about 1½ cups, including fat. Strain, add the softened gelatin, and stir until it is dissolved. When the terrine is done, remove it from the oven, and pour the broth over it. Cover with foil and weight it down to keep the meat submersed. Let stand for 2 hours. Remove the weight, cover tightly and refrigerate until well chilled. Serve the terrine either in slices or as a spread with bread.

ROAST HOLIDAY GOOSE WITH APPLE AND PRUNE STUFFING

Serves 8

If you cannot find a fresh goose, there are excellent frozen ones on the market. A frozen goose should be thoroughly thawed before roasting, preferably in the refrigerator, in its original wrap, which will take 1½ to 2 days. There is a great deal of fat on a goose. Therefore it should be roasted slowly and on a rack so that the bird crisps while the fat drips down into the roasting pan. Reserve the fat for future cooking; it can be used for many dishes.

8- to 10-pound goose
½ cup finely chopped onion
6 tablespoons butter
5 to 6 cups fresh bread crumbs
2 teaspoons salt
1 cup cooked peeled chestnuts
    or canned chestnuts
2 cups peeled and chopped apples
1 cup chopped prunes, steeped in hot
    water or Madeira until puffed
½ teaspoon nutmeg
1 teaspoon thyme

Remove any excess fat from the cavity of the goose. Also remove the neck and giblets, and use to prepare a broth while the goose is roasting.

Sauté the onion lightly in the butter and add the bread crumbs. Toss to moisten throughout. Add the rest of the ingredients, and blend well. Stuff the goose with this mixture, and truss; or just skewer the cavity and tie the legs together. Place breast side up on a rack in a roasting pan. Roast for

55

1 hour at 400°, then prick the skin all over with a fork to release the fat. Reduce the temperature to 350° and roast for another hour, without basting. As the fat is rendered, remove it from the roasting pan and reserve. After the second hour, test the bird to see if it is done. It should be well browned, the leg meat should be soft when pressed, and the juices should run clear with the faintest blush of pink when the thigh is pricked. If more cooking is required, reduce the heat to 325° and continue roasting. The total cooking time will be from 2 to 2½ hours. Remove the goose from the oven and allow to stand for 15 minutes before carving.

If you like, degrease the pan juices and thicken with flour, arrowroot or cornstarch to make a sauce.

PHEASANT
AND QUAIL

PHEASANT WITH SAUERKRAUT

Serves 2

Sauerkraut and cabbage seem to have a special affinity for certain game birds that makes for a remarkable blending of flavors.

2 pounds sauerkraut
2 cups chicken broth
1 cup white wine
8 crushed juniper berries
½ teaspoon caraway seeds
1 pheasant, singed and cleaned
4 tablespoons butter
Salt and freshly ground black pepper

Wash the sauerkraut under cold running water in a colander, let drain, and squeeze lightly to dispose of excess liquid. Place it in a deep casserole. Pour in the broth and wine, and add the juniper berries and caraway seeds. Cover and bake for 1 hour in a 350° oven.

Meanwhile melt the butter in a skillet and brown the pheasant on all sides to color evenly. Sprinkle with salt and pepper. Place it in the casserole in the bed of sauerkraut. Cover and bake again at 350° for 45 minutes to an hour, until the bird is tender. Serve on a hot platter surrounded by the sauerkraut and fried hominy squares.

PHEASANT PIONEER STYLE

Serves 4 to 6

A favorite pheasant dish served in the Beard home when he was a child. "It is simple," he writes, "but I have never had pheasant that tasted better no matter how elaborately prepared. Sometimes I make one change in the original recipe, substituting butter for bacon fat. I've never decided which I like better."

2 pheasants, well cleaned
6 slices good smoked bacon (not the limp, tasteless variety)
Flour seasoned with salt and pepper
3 tablespoons flour
1½ cups heavy cream

Cut the pheasants into quarters or disjoint them as you would a chicken. Dredge the pieces in seasoned flour. Sauté the bacon in a large skillet until crisp. Remove from the pan and keep warm. Brown the pheasant in the bacon fat, turning the pieces to cook them evenly. Reduce the heat, cover the pan, and simmer for about 15 minutes or until the pheasant is tender. Uncover, increase the heat, and cook for a minute or so more to crisp the skin side of the pheasant. Remove to a hot platter and garnish with the bacon strips.

Pour off all but 3 tablespoons of the fat in the pan, and add the 3 tablespoons of flour. Blend well over moderate heat, and gradually stir in the heavy cream. Continue stirring until the sauce thickens. Season the sauce to taste and serve with the sautéed pheasant.

ROAST PHEASANT WITH BLACK CHERRIES

Serves 2

The pheasant can be stuffed with a savory bread crumb mixture or with celery, parsley, and onion; or just place a tablespoon of butter in the cavity.

1 young pheasant
4 slices bacon
4 ounces rum
Salt and freshly ground black pepper
1 cup canned black cherries, drained

Singe and clean the pheasant, and stuff or leave plain. Lay the strips of bacon over the breast. Place in a roasting pan, and roast for 50 minutes at 350°, basting every 10 minutes with fat from the pan. Remove from the oven, pour off the fat, and strip off the bacon. Pour half the rum over the bird, and set ablaze. When the flame has died out, sprinkle the bird with salt and pepper. Add the cherries and remaining rum to the pan, and heat for 3 or 4 minutes. Serve the pheasant on a platter with the cherries and well-browned hominy squares.

ROAST QUAIL

Quail is available fresh from specialty meat and game markets and is also sold frozen in many stores and by mail-order suppliers. These little birds weigh only ⅔ to ¾ of a pound and cannot take much cooking, but they lend themselves to a variety of preparations. This method is as good as any.

6 quail, split down the back
and cleaned (reserve the giblets)
Dijon mustard
12 slices bacon
Salt and freshly ground black pepper
3 tablespoons butter
Cognac
6 slices hot toast

Brush the breasts and legs of the quail with a fairly heavy coat of Dijon mustard. Lay a slice of bacon over the skin side of each half, covering the legs, thighs, and breast sections. Arrange on the rack of a broiler pan, and sprinkle lightly with salt and pepper. Roast at 450° for 19 to 21 minutes. Do not overcook.

While the quail are roasting sauté the livers, hearts, and gizzards in the butter until just cooked. Season them with salt, pepper, and a touch of cognac. Chop very fine.

Butter the toast well and then spread with a thin film of Dijon mustard. Add a layer of chopped giblets. Serve each quail on a piece of toast, and spoon over any juices from the sautéed giblets. Serve 1 quail per person as a first course or 2 as a main course.

Roast Quail Stuffed
with Oysters

FOR EACH QUAIL:

4 to 6 oysters, freshly shucked

2 tablespoons butter

Thin slice of lemon

Salt and freshly ground black pepper

Barding fat

Stuff each quail with the oysters, butter, and lemon, and add a bit of salt and pepper. Tie barding fat around the breast. Place on a rack in a shallow roasting pan and roast at 450° for 20 minutes. Remove the barding fat, baste with the pan juices, and sprinkle with salt and pepper. Roast for another 5 to 6 minutes, basting again. Serve on an oval of well buttered toasted bread. Serves 1 as a first course.